Schaum
Christmas Cameos
Level Six

T0056024

A set of distinctive piano transcriptions by John W. Schaum

Foreword

The music portrays a wide range of emotions subject to individual interpretation. The performer is free to play at different tempos or with rubato, according to personal taste. Likewise, dynamic inflections and pedaling may be added or altered.

The arrangements are suitable for performance in recitals and church programs. If desired, many of the pieces could be combined to make an attractive medley.

*Additional Cameo books at <u>Level 6</u>: *More Christmas Cameos* (#1112) and *Still More Christmas Cameos* (#1113).

Performance CD available featuring John W. Schaum playing all selections from this book, Christmas Cameos, Level 6 and More Christmas Cameos (#3003).

Angels We Have Heard On High 21
Away In a Manger 11
The First Noel 2
Good King Wenceslas 7
Hark! The Herald Angels Sing 20
It Came Upon the Midnight Clear 14
Joy To the World 12
Lo, How a Rose E'er Blooming 15
O Come All Ye Faithful (Adeste Fideles) 8
O Holy Night (Cantique De Noel) 16
O Little Town of Bethlehem 6
Once in Royal David's City 19
O Sanctissima (O How Joyfully) 22
Silent Night 3
We Three Kings of Orient Are 4
What Child Is This? (Greensleeves) 10

EXCLUSIVELY DISTRIBUTED BY

HAL•LEONARD®
CORPORATION
7777 W. BLUEMOUND RD. P.O. BOX 13819 MILWAUKEE, WI 53213

© Copyright 1959, Renewed 1987 by Schaum Publications, Inc., Mequon, Wisconsin
International Copyright Secured • All Rights Reserved • Printed in U.S.A.

ISBN: 978-1-62906-037-8

The First Noel

Traditional
Arr. by John W. Schaum

Silent Night

Joseph Mohr

Franz Gruber
Arr. by John W. Schaum

We Three Kings of Orient Are*

J. H. Hopkins, Jr.
Arr. by John W. Schaum

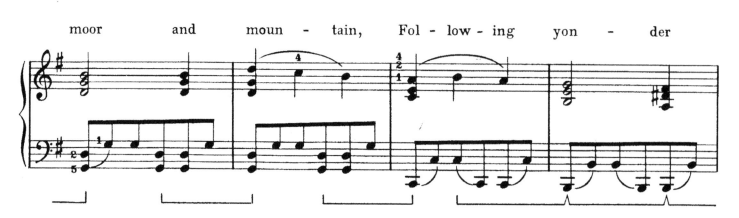

*NOTE: This arrangement is in the style of the Arabian Dance from the Tchaikowsky "Nutcracker Suite."

O Little Town of Bethlehem

Phillips Brooks

Lewis H. Redner
Arr. by John W. Schaum

Good King Wenceslas

John Mason Neale

Traditional Carol
Arr. by John W. Schaum

O Come All Ye Faithful

(ADESTE FIDELES)

Frederick Oakeley

Latin Hymn
Arr. by John W. Schaum

What Child is This

(GREENSLEEVES)

William C. Dix

Old English Air
Arr. by John W. Schaum

Away in a Manger

Of German Origin
Arr. by John W. Schaum

Anonymous

Joy to the World

Rev. Isaac Watts

G. F. Handel
Arr. by   John W. Schaum

ev' - ry heart pre - pare Him

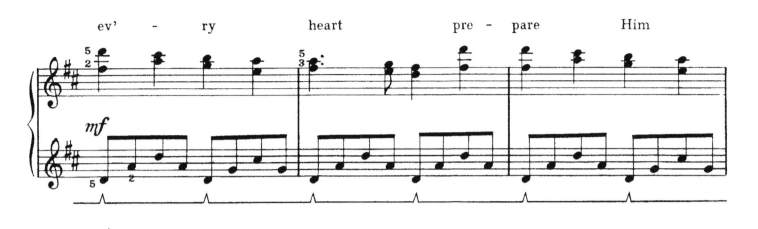

room And heav'n and na - ture sing, And

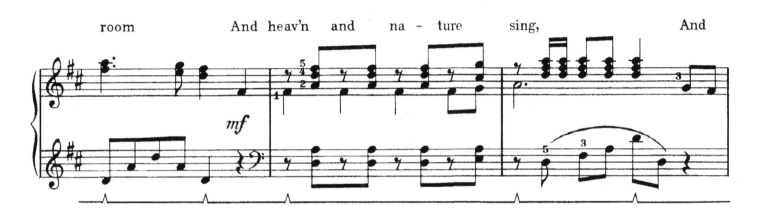

heav'n and na - ture sing, And heav'n, and

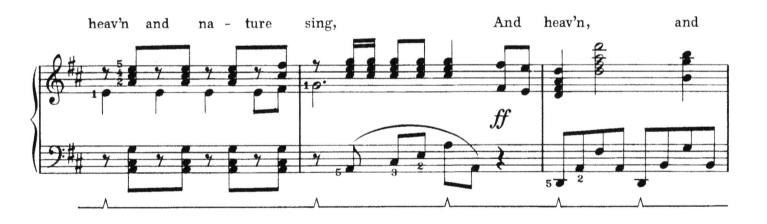

heav'n and na - ture sing.

It Came Upon the Midnight Clear

Rev. Edmund A. Sears

(NOCTURNE)

Richard S. Willis
Arr. by John W. Schaum

Lo, How a Rose E'er Blooming

Dr. Theodore Baker

M. Praetorius
Arr. by John W. Schaum

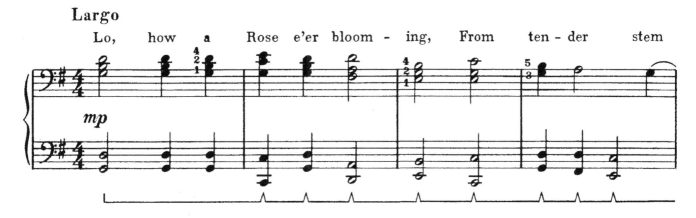

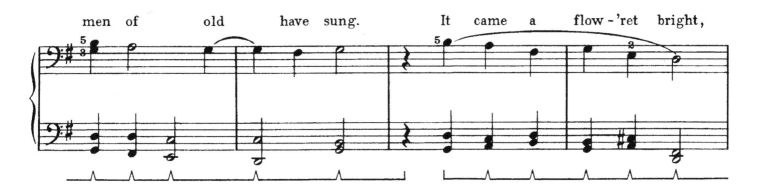

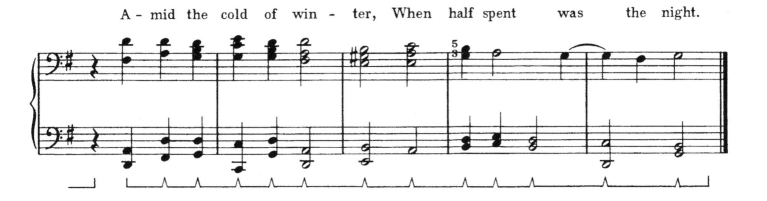

O Holy Night

(CANTIQUE DE NOEL)

A. Adam
Arr. by John W. Schaum

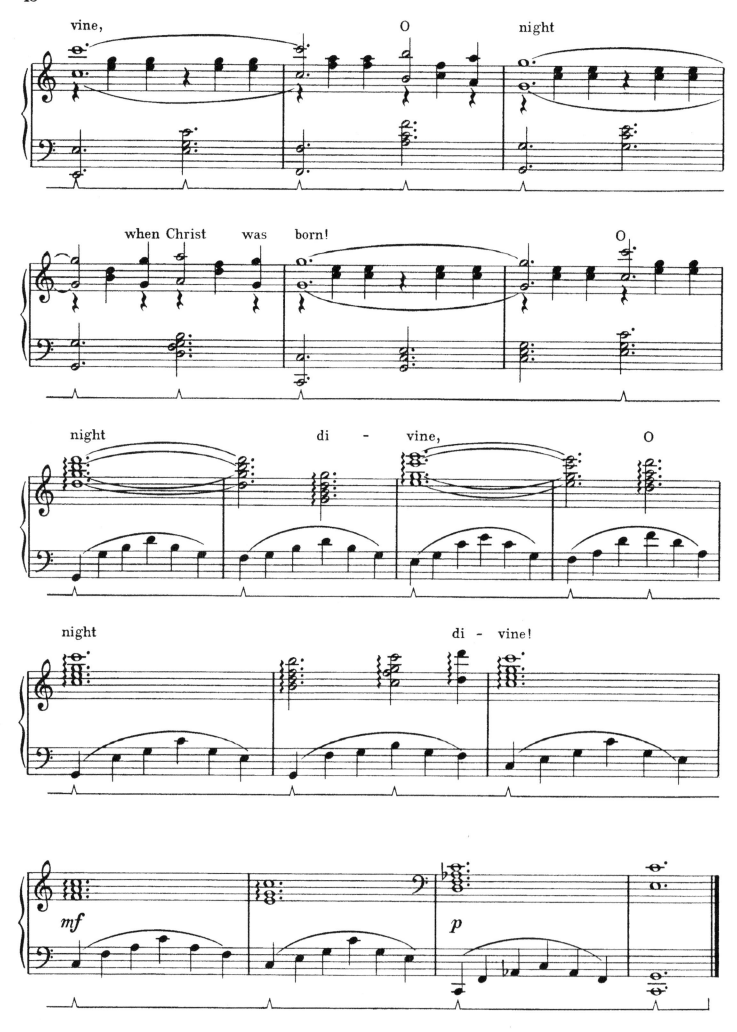

Once in Royal David's City

H. J. Gauntlett

C. F. Alexander
Arr. by John W. Schaum

Hark! The Herald Angels Sing

Charles Wesley

F. Mendelssohn
Arr. by John W. Schaum

Angels We Have Heard on High

Traditional French Carol
Arr. by John W. Schaum

O Sanctissima

(O HOW JOYFULLY)

Sicilian Hymn
Arr. by John W. Schaum

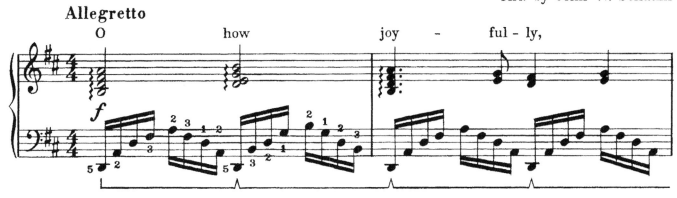

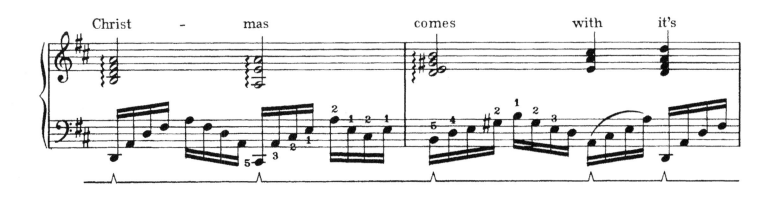

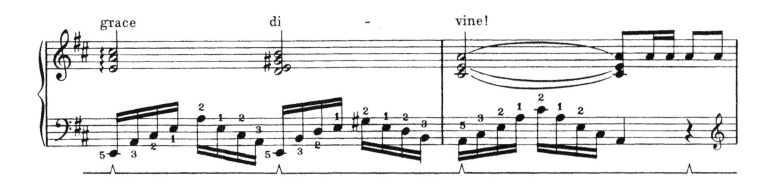